a year in the life of **the duddon valley** bill birkett

FRANCES LINCOLN

a year in the life of the duddon valley bill birkett

Many thanks
To my family – Sue my wife, Rowan my daughter, William my son –
for great days in the Duddon. To Dave Birkett for his knowledge of fell
life and crags. To the Wrights – Pat, Dave, James and John – for walking
with me. To Richard Bowness for angling and fish expertise. To all the
very many climbers and companions I've shared days on the hills with.
For climbing with me and being photographed: Tony Greenbank,
Al Phizacklea and George and Anna Sharpe. George Birkett for
local knowledge and advice on the ways of the salmon. John Birkett
for local folklore. To the locals of the Duddon. Paul Batten, landlord of
the Newfield Inn. To some fine little publications giving an insight into
the history of the valley: Felicity Hughes, *William Wordsworth and
Wonderful Walker*; B. S. Wignall Simpson, *A Mountain Chapelry in
Cumbria*; G. K. Stebbens, *Bygone Folk and Industries of the Duddon
Valley*; J. C. Cooper, *Duddon Valley History*; all are available from
Ulpha Post Office and Stores. To my mates in the SOGs (Sad Old Gits):
Mark Squires and George Sharpe. To John Nicoll and Kate Cave of
Frances Lincoln for having faith enough to publish this book. To Jane
Havell for producing a fine blend of the material. To those protective
bodies and groups who care about the Duddon and seek to protect
its unique character and beauty: the National Trust, the National Park
Authority, the Countryside Commission, English Heritage and the
Friends of the Lake District.

Bill Birkett Photo Library
Bill Birkett has an extensive photographic library covering all of
Britain's mountains and wild places including one of the most
comprehensive collections of photographs of the English Lake District.
For photographic commissions, information, prints or library images
telephone 015394 37420, mobile 07789 304 949, or
e-mail bill.birkett1@btopenworld.com

*TITLE PAGE: Ice along the ancient high-level route of Park Head Road,
now a rough track, rises from Kiln Bank Cross to flank the rocky
independent top of Brock Barrow (left of the stone wall). Beyond the
col, by Brock Barrow, it drops beneath the shapely high cone of Caw
to offer stunning open views across Seathwaite, Wallowbarrow and
the mid Duddon.*

Frances Lincoln Limited
4 Torriano Mews
Torriano Avenue
London NW5 2RZ

A Year in the Life of the Duddon Valley
Copyright © 2006 Frances Lincoln Limited

Text and photographs copyright © 2006 Bill Birkett
Map on page 6 by Martin Bagness
Edited and designed by Jane Havell Associates

First Frances Lincoln edition 2006

Bill Birkett has asserted his moral right to be identified as Author of this
Work in accordance with the Copyright, Designs and Patents Act 1988

British Library cataloguing-in-publication data
A catalogue record for this book is available from the British Library

ISBN 10: 0 7112 2637 7
ISBN 13: 978 0 7112 2637 1

Printed in Singapore

contents

the duddon valley introduction

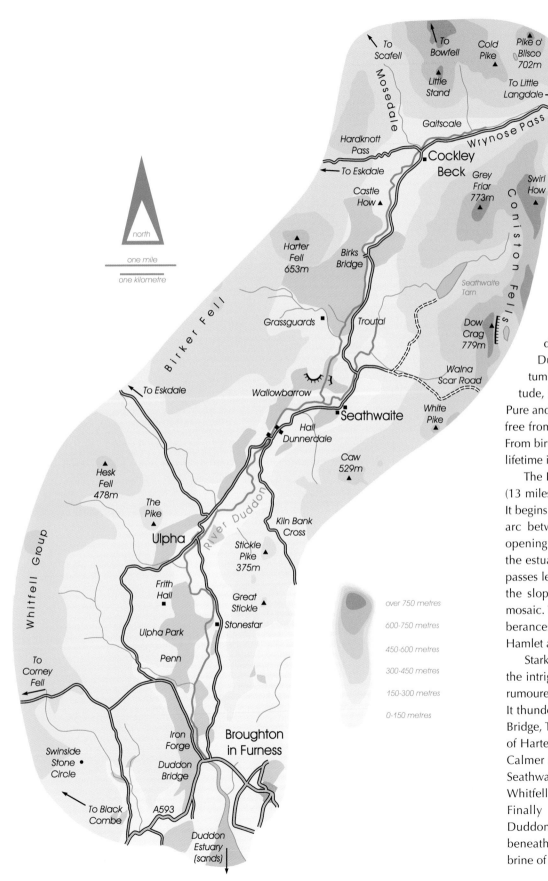

To Scafell

To Bowfell

Cold Pike ▲

Pike o' Blisco 702m ▲

Mosedale

Little Stand ▲

Gaitscale

To Little Langdale →

Wrynose Pass

Hardknott Pass

Cockley Beck ■

Grey Friar 773m ▲

Swirl How ▲

← To Eskdale

Coniston Fells

Castle How ▲

Harter Fell 653m ▲

Birks Bridge

Seathwaite Tarn

Dow Crag 779m ▲

north

one mile

one kilometre

Grassguards ■

Troutal

Walna Scar Road

Birker Fell

Wallowbarrow

Seathwaite ■

White Pike ▲

← To Eskdale

Hall Dunnerdale

Caw 529m ▲

Hesk Fell 478m ▲

The Pike ▲

Ulpha

River Duddon

Kiln Bank Cross

Stickle Pike 375m ▲

Whitfell Group

Frith Hall ■

Great Stickle ▲

Ulpha Park

Stonestar ■

Penn

To Corney Fell

Iron Forge

Broughton in Furness

Swinside Stone Circle •

Duddon Bridge

To Black Combe

A593

Duddon Estuary (sands)

over 750 metres

600-750 metres

450-600 metres

300-450 metres

150-300 metres

0-150 metres

There is a point somewhere above the Three Shires Stone where a raindrop splattering on the rocks will divide – some will flow down the Duddon and some down the Langdales. So close, yet a world apart. The Duddon, with its elfin woods, crystal clear rock pools, tumbling waterfalls, rocky steeps and, above all else, solitude, beguiles and enchants like no other Lakeland valley. Pure and joyous, uncompromised by lake or tarn, it flows carefree from the heights to the sea in an ever-changing journey. From birth to death, uniquely within the Lake District, its entire lifetime is cradled within the magic of the fells.

The Duddon's is a surprisingly long journey, some 21 km (13 miles) from source to sea, with many changes in character. It begins at the head of Wrynose Pass, to strike a south-westerly arc between shapely fells and wooded slopes, alternately opening and closing, before finally narrowing to emerge into the estuary below Duddon Bridge. Along the way, numerous passes lead through breaks in the hills. Hanging valleys pierce the slopes, picturesque farms and stone houses add to the mosaic. Woods and grazing pasture come and go, rocky protuberances stand defiant, waterfalls crash and deep pools laze. Hamlet and village appear and disappear.

Stark and naked along Wrynose Bottom, the Duddon passes the intriguing ruins of Gaitscale, where the sheep of old were rumoured to have an extra rib and the Roman legions marched. It thunders through the rocky, tree-encrusted narrows of Birks Bridge, Troutal and Wallowbarrow Gorges, under the influence of Harter Fell to the west and the Coniston massif to the east. Calmer and deeper, though just as beguiling, it flows below Seathwaite and through Hall Dunnerdale and Ulpha with the Whitfell hills to the west and the Dow Crag group to the east. Finally it rolls through the wonderful daffodil woods by Duddon Hall and the ancient ironworks before slipping beneath the stone arches of Duddon Bridge to join with the brine of Duddon Sands.

Lying outside the Lake District National Park boundary, the Duddon Sands estuary reaches for some further 18 km (11 miles) before joining the Irish Sea. It runs beside the Furness Peninsula to the south: Askam, Barrrow and the whale's tail of Walney Island and the fells of Kirby Moor. Millom and Haverigg, overlooked by mighty Blackcombe, lie to the north. A significant, though largely forgotten, world of water ebbing and flowing over shifting sands, it receives a regular assemblage of over 20,000 wintering waterfowl, waders and seabirds. During severe winters, numbers may exceed 70,000. They include the shelduck, red-breasted merganser, oyster-catcher, ringed plover, dunlin and curlew.

In the upper reaches of the valley, Herdwick sheep roam from fell to valley bottom before stone walls and fences take over. Cattle graze near Cockley Beck and spring lambs gambol in the meadows by the roadside. Deer, raven, buzzard and peregrine falcon are frequent sightings, but the red squirrel is in severe decline. Meadows, cut for hay in summertime, dot the valley bottom. During springtime the woods are aflower with primroses, violets, daffodils, bluebells and wood anemones.

As witnessed by the nearby Swinside (Sunkenkirk) Stone Circle and the polished Langdale stone axes found in the sands of Walney Island – both thought to be Neolithic in age (c. 5000–3000 BC) – the Duddon Valley has long been used and occupied by man. Ancient cairns and bloomeries, possibly of the Iron Age, litter the landscape around the Dunnerdale and Stonestar area of low fells, while numerous copper workings and nearby burial mounds indicate a strong occupation throughout the Bronze Age. The Romans left their road, with its construction of carefully laid cobbles still intact in places along Wrynose Bottom, on their march from west to east.

To those Norsemen taking the short sea journey from their stronghold on the Isle of Man, with their shallow-drafted long-boats slipping easily upstream from estuary to river, the Duddon Valley must have seemed like the promised land. From the sea, the narrow entrance to the dale is elusive, secretive and tantalising, hidden among the folds of the fells and clad by trees. Yet, while the presence of the valley is only hinted at from the estuary, the hills inveigle. The shapely cone-like protuberances of Stickle Pike and Caw, the striking pyramidal form of Harter Fell, and the high rocky massif of the Scafells beyond must have borne a striking resemblance to the Norsemen's native lands. Beyond the entrance they would have found fertile, sheltered grazing, woods, extensive high pasture and a relatively mild climate, not to mention that irresistible Duddon charm. No wonder the Tynwald Viking parliament held sway for four and a half centuries, from 800 to 1266. Perhaps, judging by the local dialect of the hill farmers, they never really left.

In the twelfth and thirteenth centuries, the monks of Furness worked these lands and manufactured iron here; they were probably the first to exploit the huge haematite deposits found within the limestone of the Furness Peninsula and beneath Duddon Sands. Later Frith Hall was built, complete with Peel Tower, in a dominant postion high above Ulpha Common. Serving as an inn in the eighteenth century, it was the site of foul murder before falling into ruin. Around this time, slate quarrying, copper mining, charcoal burning, bobbin manufacture and the smelting of iron all came to prominence. The amazingly complete remains of Duddon Bridge Ironworks, built in 1736, show that it was one of the most important blast furnaces of its day.

The Tour

Today most visitors enter the Duddon at its head via Wrynose Pass from Little Langdale and leave, after briefly traversing Wrynose Bottom, via Hardknott Pass into Eskdale. They have experienced but a mere glimpse of this intriguing dale. For those who appreciate the quiet charm and air of solitude that pervade the remaining length of the Duddon this may be a good thing, for the twisting narrow road, often flanked by stone

ABOVE: As evening falls, a glint of silver shining through the darkness marks the course of Cockley Beck along Wrynose Bottom.

walls and punctuated with blind bends, was never meant for modern vehicular transport.

The flattish base of Wrynose Bottom, wedged between the slopes of Little Stand to the north and Hell's Gill Pike to the south, framed by the majesty of Harter Fell to the west and the high mountain pass to the east, can adopt a number of aspects. Stones litter a treeless landscape. Long, coarse fell grasses predominate. When the sun shines, Wrynose Bottom appears warm and welcoming; without it, wild and bleak. Running alongside the road the beck tumbles on a jumble of rounded cobbles by rocky outcrops and through pools dammed by banks of shilla (shingle) before meandering away to return by Cockley Beck Bridge. Looking at this slight watercourse, a mere trickle during the heat of summer, it is difficult to believe that sea trout still run all the way to the rocky waterfalls beneath Wrynose Pass. And hard to accept, looking over to the ruins of Gaitscale and the mainly hidden remnants of the Roman road traversing the opposite banks of the beck, that once this empty landscape bustled with life.

The sycamores, whitewashed farmhouse and stone-arched bridge of Cockley Beck always appear welcoming. Above, to the north, Mosedale rises to a view of the distant Scafells. Once a main trackway, leading between the heights of Bowfell and Esk Pike via Ore Gap to descend to Angle Tarn at the head of Borrowdale, it is now used infrequently by hillwalkers and climbers. The road over Hardknott Pass departs westwards at this point and suddenly, below Cockley Beck, the nature of the dale becomes somehow friendlier and more intimate.

Recently partially fenced, the road used to run unguarded through the meadow and alongside the Duddon beneath the rocky stand of Castle How. The road does a double right angle to pass between the buildings of the old farm of Dale Head (now used by Leeds University) before the conifers of Dunnerdale Forest make an impact on the scenery. A loop around Hinning House leads to the new Birks Bridge, complete with car park,

and, a little further downstream, the old stone-arched Birks Bridge. From the latter a now abandoned track leads to the old farm of the same name. From the former a forestry road leads to the small community of Grassguards which stands hidden among the folds of the hillside to the west. The road continues to wind by Troutal Farm before skirting the deep, hidden and heavily wooded Wallowbarrow Gorge. Beyond Seathwaite Bridge, crossing Tarn Beck which has arisen from the reservoir of Seathwaite Tarn, a road splits off south to rise to the high and rocky Walna Scar road. This leads over the mountains to Coniston; the route is officially classified as a road, but it is steep and rough and definitely not suitable for cars.

A little further and descent is made into a world of mixed, though predominantly oak, woods and craggy outcrops. Above to the left lies Turner Hall Farm and its idyllic campsite. By the road Tarn Beck crashes through a series of rock slides, channels and waterfalls before calming itself beside Seathwaite Church. Although Tarn Beck has not yet joined the River Duddon, this happens just downstream of Seathwaite village, which lies at the heart of the valley.

Seathwaite is so slight that the term village may seem perhaps too grandiose to describe it. Nevertheless the main cluster of buildings, strung along the narrow road, offers a perfect composition. It consists of an inn and, separated by a hundred yards and a right-angled bend, a village hall, vicarage and church – and little else. But first impressions are deceptive, for scattered in secretive nooks and dells, among the woods, craggy outcrops and occasionally flat fields can be found cottages and farms – a rustic idyll, little changed for centuries. Hereabouts, and all along the Duddon, through woods of incandescent colour in autumn, are low-level walks suitable in most conditions. On a higher plane, though not yet the highest, are wild moors and craggy steeps. Above all towers the Coniston range of hills, as accessible from here as from Coniston, and to the west the pyramidal Harter Fell.

ABOVE LEFT: Sycamore leaves gather in the rock pools beneath the stone arch of Cockley Beck Bridge. Sea trout and salmon, once in considerable numbers, wait here for the autumn rains to swell the waters to sufficient depth to allow them passage through the rocky rapids.

ABOVE: The whitewashed, traditional, stone-built Cockley Beck Farmhouse offers self-catering and bed-and-breakfast accommodation in a remote setting. It remains a working farm, with a large area of upland fell grazing under its management.

ABOVE: Beneath the trig point on the summit rocks of Caw, this inscription shows that 'JC', possibly having walked barefoot over the waters of the Duddon Estuary, visited the region in 1870. I am sure he was not disappointed: the beauty in every direction is nothing short of wondrous. Miraculously little has changed since.

ABOVE RIGHT: Below Buck Barrow and high above Logan Beck Bridge, a frozen mountain pond lies on the flats of Plough Fell. Even such minutiae has beauty in and around the Duddon.

Maps tell you there are two Seathwaites in the Lake District, this and its famous namesake which branches off Borrowdale to provide a popular gateway to the western fells. Locals know different! In fact, the latter is 'Seawaite' and this is 'Seathat'. In Seathat the inn and the church have particular prominence – just how it should be in any civilised society.

Prior to the inn opening, the village vicar, a true country parson and a remarkable character, brewed and sold his own ale. Known as 'Wonderful' Walker, he was truly an exceptional man. Born in 1709 at Under Crag Farm in Seathat, he was the youngest of twelve children. Considered too weak for proper work, he was encouraged to be a scholar. He rose to be schoolmaster at Loweswater before becoming curate at Seathat when he was 26. In his spare time, apart from his brewing activities, he ran his own smallholding, jobbed for other farmers, spun wool, made his own clothing, cut his own peat for the fire, made his own rushlights, cured the sick, fed the poor, acted as a lawyer, and wrote and read for the illiterate. With his wife Ann he raised a large family. His stipend was £5 per year, yet on his death aged 93 he left what was then a fortune of £2,000. He and his wife are buried in the churchyard.

William and Dorothy Wordsworth stayed at the Newfield Inn in Seathat in September 1804, two years after the death of Robert 'Wonderful' Walker, and they were so impressed by his remarkable story that William subsequently included references to the curate in his long poem 'The Excursion' (1814) and in his sequence of thirty-four sonnets 'The River Duddon' (1820). He even included a memoir of Walker in the notes appended to the sonnets: 'such a sense of his various excellences was prevalent in the country, that the ephithet of WONDERFUL is to this day attached to his name'. In 'The Excursion' (Book VII) Wordsworth wrote:

These titles emperors and chiefs have borne,
Honour assumed or given: and him, the WONDERFUL,
Our simple shepherds, speaking from the heart,
Deservedly have styled. – From his abode
In a dependent chapelry that lies
Beyond yon hill, a poor and rugged wild,
Which in his soul he lovingly embraced,
And, having once espoused, would never quit;
Into its graveyard will ere long be borne
That lowly, great, good Man.

However, it hasn't all been peace and tranquillity in little Seathat. On 25 July 1904, a gang of navvies, laid off from building the dam compounding Seathwaite Tarn, held a riot centred on the Newfield Inn. After a very heavy drinking session, they took exception to being asked to leave. Having been thrown out, they smashed windows around the village before returning, whereupon landlord Thomas Dawson, after due warning, blasted them with his shotgun. Three fell and one, Owen Kavanagh, died from his wounds the following day. Thomas Dawson was taken to court, charged with murder, but the magistrate ruled that it had been self-defence during riotous assembly and dismissed the case.

Down the road a little way is Hall Dunnerdale where a road branches off over Kiln Bank to the real Dunnerdale and so to Broughton Mills. Our way, however, leads over Hall Bridge and on to Ulpha. Here, on 19 August 1936, James Dawson caught a 43-inch, 26lb salmon, the outline of which is still etched on top of the wall if you know where to look. Before reaching the centre of Ulpha a road, climbing steeply to cross the wilds of Birker Fell before dropping into Eskdale, leads off to the right. At its base is a wooden building, the now forgotten village hall once used for hunt balls, and above it the former Traveller's Rest Inn, now converted into flats.

The name Ulpha arguably comes from Old Norse *ulfhauga*, 'wolf hill'. Here can be found a combination post office and village store, the church of St John the Baptist and, over

Ulpha Bridge, the former school building (closed in 1999). The church was restored in the nineteenth century but retains some earlier wall paintings. The entrance is marked by a slate-roofed lych gate; two impressive bells hang above the gable. Wordsworth wrote of the church:

The Kirk of Ulpha to the pilgrim's eye
Is welcome as a star, that doth present
Its shining forehead through the peaceful rent
Of a black cloud diffused o'er half the sky . . .
How sweet were leisure! could it yield no more
Than 'mid that wave-washed Churchyard to recline,
From pastoral graves extracting thoughts divine;
Or there to pace, and mark the summits hoar
Of distant moon-lit mountains faintly shine,
Soothed by the unseen River's gentle roar.

Before the bridge a minor road heads off to pass the old bobbin mill beneath Millbrow, rising past Old Hall Farm and dropping again by Logan Beck, before joining the road over Corney Fell which leads in turn to the main west coast road just south of Muncaster Castle. Our route crosses the bridge to traverse Ulpha Common, Whistling Green and further open common land beside the river. This is a favourite picnic location with ancient ironworks, presumably old bloomery sites, hidden among the thick bracken and rocky knolls that form the side of Cinder Hill above to the west.

With the high knolls of the Pike above Ulpha, and Penn, standing to the west looking down on Ulpha Park, the valley closes and narrows for the last time. The road leaves the river and rises, with the gaunt remains of Frith Hall framed on the skyline, to pass beneath Stonestar Crag and on past Whineray Ground and Rawfold, with Duddon Hall and the daffodil woods below. Finally, a steep descent to sea level is made down Bank End to intercept the west coast road by the end of Duddon Bridge. On the other side of the bridge are the ancient Duddon Bridge Ironworks and the road leading over Corney Fell. You can drive down either side of the estuary – though to appreciate it best I would recommend a shallow-drafted longboat.

ABOVE: A small Post Office and general store stands near the centre of Ulpha. A mine of information and local knowledge, it sells maps, local history and guide books. A section through the door on the right has free tourist information and leaflets (open outside shop hours). Unfortunately the inn and the school are now closed, but the deep pool below Ulpha Bridge is a favourite swimming venue open to all during the summer months.

OPPOSITE: Looking up the estuary of Duddon Sands from Dunnerholme Point at high tide, the secretive entrance to the Duddon Valley lies to the left. The prominent, shapely cone is Stickle Pike (which has a close resemblance to its Langdale namesake), framed by the mighty Scafells beyond. Visiting Vikings would have seen this same view.

walna scar slate

In old documents the quarry was called 'Walney' Scar; it is known to have been worked since at least 1757 though it is likely to be much older. The slate found here is a metamorphosed rock of volcanic/sedimentary origin. It is formed from ash and dust spewed from ancient volcanoes which have settled, probably to the bottom of a crater lake, to form a fine-grained bed of material. At Walna Scar, different types of ash have formed distinctly different beds of material, one upon the other. These differ in colour, composition and thickness, to form a distinct and attractive banded rock.

Subsequently the beds have been changed and hardened with heat and pressure, and folded by earth movements into large domes of rock. Now the special property of the slate is that is splits in straight lines, exhibiting 'slatey cleavage' along a distinct plane of weakness. These cleavage lines radiate through the rock from the centre point of the fold (or dome). When pressure is applied through the fine point of a quarryman's chisel, the slate splits along these lines. The process, known as 'riving', is one of the most skilled crafts of slate quarrying. With sufficient strength, skill and precision of eye, craftsmen can split huge slabs of material into thin plates of rock – the roofing slates that waterproof all traditional stone-built Lakeland homes. My father was a quarryman and started as an apprentice 'river'.

At Walna Scar, uniquely within the Lake District, the parallel layered bands of ash lie at a perfect right angle to the cleavage. This means that when the slate is split the different coloured bands are seen as parallel horizontal layers. The effect is visually stunning when it is used in suitable ornamental work, typically as flags in stone flooring.

RIGHT: Looking out from a 'closehead' (large underground chamber) within the extensive Walna Scar quarries. The extensive spoil heaps can be seen high on the flanks of White Pike above Seathwaite. The workings, extensive and complex, operated on many different levels, with underground and surface workings interconnected by a series of tunnels and shafts. Ruined buildings abound. Amid the spoil heaps are the remains of living quarters and the 'home farm', where the quarrymen lived during the week, sustained by their own produce, poultry and livestock.

OPPOSITE TOP LEFT: A fragment of the unique Walna Scar slate lies broken on the Walna Scar Road. Although still classed as a public road, the high track over Walna Scar is now unsuitable for motor vehicles. Once it served as an important highway through the mountains, providing direct access to Coniston and linking the numerous slate quarries on both the Coniston and Duddon sides of the high dividing hills.

OPPOSITE TOP RIGHT: A masterpiece: the stone-flagged floor of the Newfield Inn is made from Walna Scar banded slate, unique within the Lake District. This floor has not always been so prominent – back in the 1960s it was hidden from view. There's a bit of a tale about how I first came upon it. One Saturday night I was nervously ordering one of my first pints of beer when I spotted my dad's boss, quarry owner Roly Myres, sitting on a stool at the end of the bar! I thought, 'I'm dead': my father, a strict teetotaller who was not fully attuned to the liberal attitude of the swinging 60s, would not have responded favourably to his son caught drinking underage. My fears were compounded when Roly beckoned me over. Then, to my huge surprise, he bent down, lifted the matting and showed me the slate floor, saying, 'Look at that, Bill, it's beautiful. There's no other Lakeland slate like it, and they cover it up.' I'll never forget it (and my dad never found out).

OPPOSITE: Inside a ruinous quarry building lies a long-abandoned slab of slate. Judging by its shape, it was destined to be a gatepost. Despite its unique and eye-catching qualities, most of this banded slate was used for purely functional purposes. Roofing slates were the main product, along with gateposts, lintels, building coigns and general masonry. Larger slabs were used in bridges, stone fences and as dividing walls in animal byres. Only a small proportion would have been used for stone floor flagging.

winter

As the sun falls behind Harter Fell, the hanging wisps of cloud and stony flanks of the not so distant Scafells turn to crimson. Among the high fells, as darkness falls, stars twinkle above the white snows of Grey Friar. In the valley below, the River Duddon weaves a silver thread through the darkness while the dog fox, in search of the vixen, howls wolf-like into the cuttingly cold air. There used to be hunt balls and village dances to brighten the winter gloom, but these have passed away. I once went over Wrynose Pass on my motorbike, with thick ice in all the gutters, and I swear the runnel cut by the snowplough was higher than my helmet.

OPPOSITE: The view from Long Top, the highest of the Crinkle Crags, looking down Mosedale and across the Duddon Valley to Caw. The shining rivulets are ice. Beyond lies the Duddon Estuary and the sweeping tail of Walney Island.

OVERLEAF: Snow plasters the fells around the head of the Duddon. Looking from Carrs, the first prominent rocky height is Little Stand, with the valleys of Mosedale branching around it to the left and Wrynose Bottom to the right. Behind we are looking end on to the Crinkle Crags and Bowfell, while the mountain massif beyond, capped by cloud, is England's highest, the Scafells.

ABOVE: Pike o' Blisco flanked by the craggy outcrops of Black Crag, the source of the Duddon. Just visible, hanging in the basin top left, is Red Tarn, whose waters flow into Great Langdale. The incredible rough rhyolite volcanic rocks of Black Crag, pitted by plaque-like formations and gas pockets, is a favourite climbing venue in the summer months. Pike o' Blisco, easily approached from the Three Shires Stone at the head of Wrynose Pass, offers the hillwalker extensive views down the Duddon, valley and estuary, which under favourable conditions extend to the far distant hills of North Wales.

OPPOSITE TOP: Over the banks of the River Duddon, the stark and ragged edge of Dunnerdale Forest, thinned by wind and felling, makes for a forlorn sight. I am not a fan of ranked conifers, which markedly suppress the natural flora and fauna. Amid this intricate, diverse landscape they seem particularly alien.

OPPOSITE LEFT: Overshadowed by leafless trees, pack-ice reminiscent of the Arctic wastes gathers in the last leg of the Duddon, a result of heavy overnight snow followed by a rapid thaw. Beyond is the Duddon Bridge which marks the high-tide boundary of the estuary.

OPPOSITE RIGHT: A murder of crows gathers atop this leafless tree near Low Whineray Ground. Below, softened by ethereal mists, the Duddon lies fringed by trees. Beyond it, at the edge of the white plain, rises the darkness of Low Park wood.

OPPOSITE TOP: Thanks to its Ancient Monument status and restoration in the 1970s, the Duddon Iron Furnace, built in 1736, remains an impressive cluster of integrated and once highly functional buildings. It is hailed as one of the most impressive charcoal-fired blast furnaces in Britain. It remained in continuous production for a hundred and thirty years until coke superseded charcoal, finally closing in 1867. This was an ideal site for iron production, with all essential elements to hand – a waterwheel (now gone), driven by water from the Duddon, powered two huge bellows blowing oxygen into the blast furnace; nearby woods supplied the charcoal. Shallow-drafted sloops delivered the iron ore from the nearby ironfields of Furness via the Duddon Estuary, right up to wharves just below Duddon Bridge. Boats transported the finished iron to where it was required, notably the great ship-building ports of Chepstow and Bristol. Charcoal and iron ore were heated to a very high temperature (1,500°C) so that the carbon in the charcoal combined with the oxygen in the ore, leaving molten, almost pure, iron. To achieve such a high temperature, a furnace stack and internal tapering furnace shaft were required to increase the blast – these are evident on the right side of the buildings.

OPPOSITE BELOW: Near the buildings of Dale Head, sheep crowd around a feeding block essential for their survival when lying snow prevents them from grazing.

ABOVE: From the heights of Kiln Bank Cross, a lovely vista unfolds over the Duddon towards Harter Fell. The snow-capped peaks right of Harter Fell are Crinkle Crags and Bowfell; to the left is Scafell. Kiln Bank Cross is the high col traversed by the road between the Duddon and Dunnerdale. It lies at the intersection of numerous ancient trackways – hence the 'cross' part of the name.

BELOW: Beyond Caw, a sea of cloud fills the Duddon Valley. This dramatic aspect looks from White Pike over Caw to the Whitfell group of hills which defines the west edge of the lower part of the dale. The isolated hill top left is Black Combe; beyond it, the bank of cloud continues unbroken across the Irish Sea.

BELOW: From Brim Fell Rake,
clouds bank impressively over
Troutal Fell and the flanks of
Grey Friar, threatening to engulf
Seathwaite Tarn. Nestling in the
folds between Dow Crag and
Grey Friar, the tarn was artificially
dammed and opened in 1910 to
serve the water needs of nearby
industrial Barrow. The remains
of ancient copper mines are
to be found above its head.
During the Second World War
a plane reputedly disappeared
beneath its surface.

ABOVE: Looking north from Caw on a cold, clear winter's day, the dark shadow-filled rift in the centre foreground is Wallowbarrow Gorge. In the middle ground stands Harter Fell, perhaps the Duddon's most influential fell, and beyond are arrayed the high Western Fells including Pillar Mountain to the left, the Scafells in the centre and Esk Pike and Bowfell to the right.

ABOVE: With the dead bracken rusty red and the hill grass the colour of burnt ochre, this view looks into the upper Duddon from the heights of Harter Fell. The white building seen in the centre is Cockley Beck Farm; above it the little hanging valley of Mosedale climbs to the left and Wrynose Bottom bends off to the right to enter the shadows.

BELOW: The summit cairn of Grey Friar silhouetted against the night sky; beyond lies the Whitfell group with the sun reflecting off the Irish Sea off Cumbria's west coast. Although there was no snow on the ground, it was late November when I took this photograph and there was plenty of ice on the path back to the Thee Shires Stone.

OPPOSITE: Lovely golden light exudes from the rapidly falling sun to fill the bottom leg of the valley between Caw and the distant mound of Black Combe. Shapely Dow Crag, top left, and lonely Seathwaite Tarn take on a steely hue as the light dims. The sands of the Duddon Estuary are visible in the centre.

ABOVE: A winter moon hangs
above the snow-clad heights of
Great Carrs, left, and Grey Friar,
right. In the base of the valley,
below Cockley Beck Farm, the
meadows remain green. This
view is from the eastern flanks
of Harter Fell.

ABOVE: A partially frozen pond on Harter Fell. The valley enclosed by the fells opposite is that of high Seathwaite Tarn on the opposite east side of the valley. Beyond are Brim Fell and Coniston Old Man, with Dow Crag just to the right.

BELOW: A storm gathers over the stand of trees on Moor How Crag, looking down the valley from below Seathwaite. The shapely little peak of The Pike can be seen beyond.

OPPOSITE: A crimson sunset fills the sky above Wrynose Bottom, looking to Harter Fell and Hardknott Pass from Wrynose Pass. Although things look set fair, with temperatures well below freezing the old rhyme 'Red sky at night, shepherd's delight' should not be relied upon by those hoping to scale the heights on the morrow.

ABOVE: The rose-coloured light of late afternoon lends a grandeur to Wallowbarrow Crag, standing large above the white buildings of High Wallowbarrow Farm. At this point the River Duddon forces its way by a series of cascades, tumbling waterfalls and rock pools through the distinct V-notch of Wallowbarrow Gorge formed by Wallowbarrow Crag to the left and Seathwaite Crags (Pen and Hollin House Tongue) to the right. Below the rocks, as the valley levels once again by Seathwaite, Tarn Beck flows in from the right to makes its confluence with the Duddon. All the woods, attractive despite their winter nakedness, are mixed deciduous consisting mostly of oak, silver birch and hazel.

OPPOSITE: Over Birks Farm, looking up the Duddon to the guardian fells of Little Stand and Cold Pike. The buildings now serve as an outdoor centre, since the planting of Dunnerdale Forest swallowed up the land once used for mixed agriculture. At the time this photograph was taken in winter 2005, most of the conifers were felled and open views prevail. The rocky knoll left of centre, beyond the larch trees, is Castle How. At the edge of the felled forest, the green grazing fields lead up past Dale Head to distant Cockley Beck.

OVERLEAF: A spectacular and angry sunset over Duddon Sands, in a view from Blawith Knott in a north-westerly direction to Millom's church steeple. The chip shop is just below the steeple and the Irish Sea beyond, though the huge ironworks, still operational in the 1960s, has now been bulldozed to the ground. Once the haematite mines, producing a particularly high-grade ore, extended out way below the estuary. My father worked as a miner here during the Second World War.

life of the buzzard

With a plentiful food supply and a wealth of nesting sites, the Duddon Valley is a particularly favourable habitat for the buzzard. Woodlands of the Duddon are among the most extensive in the Lake District and a range of woodland communities intermix with mires, meadows, craggy outcrops, heathlands and steep fellsides. Although the higher fells are heavily grazed, within the valley there is a variety of small birds, reptiles, mammals and insects, all of which are the staple diet of the predatory buzzard. Crags, rocky outcrops, trees and occasionally rough ground may all be used as nesting sites.

BELOW LEFT: This buzzard nest, an extensive pile of sticks and twigs, is lined with clean dry reeds, grass, sheep's wool and a sprig or two of juniper for good measure. It is a site that has been used successfully for many years. This year, on 9 May 2005, it contained two eggs which are non-glossy white, faintly blotched with chestnut-red streaks.

BELOW: A month later, on 8 June 2005, the eggs have hatched and there are two fluffy chicks huddled beak to tail. The chick with the wary eye is large, healthy and will survive. The other, with head hidden, is sickly and will not. That is the law of nature. It is interesting to note that the parent buzzards have completely relined the nest with fresh leaf-bearing pussy willow twigs.

OPPOSITE: Wheeling freely in the air with wings and fingers outstretched, lit by the sun, this buzzard looks almost like a golden eagle. Sometimes, especially when seen against the light, buzzards can look massive and many mistake them for eagles. However, their plaintive mewing cry, particularly when near their nest site, is a sure sign of their identity. They are much smaller, and distinctively whiter beneath, than eagles.

spring

In shower or sun, before the leaves unfurl, shining jewels of pale gold and lush emerald carpet the woods. The Duddon daffodils – quiet, slight, yet infinitely finer than the cultivated variety – are simply breathtaking. Undisturbed year after year, this celebration of youth and hope promises great things. Tree, hedge, riverbank, fellside and field all begin to stir. Waking from winter slumber, climbers tentatively probe the steeps of Wallowbarrow Crag, testing their nerve before venturing to greater heights. Louder, wilder, faster and more manic than any rock star, the green woodpecker drums for a mate. Twin buzzards, mewing plaintively, circle the sky above wood and crag. Small birds of the woodland, bush and riverbank challenge for possession of place beside the Duddon.

OPPOSITE: As the trees begin to take leaf in early May, young Herdwick lambs enjoy their first taste of spring sunshine. These meadows, below Cockley Beck with the heights of Harter Fell looking on, are filled with lambs before they are moved on to higher pastures. Only a few years ago, a road swept through the open fields – undoubtedly a statement of how infrequent the traffic used to be, though there were accidents. Today, wire fences have been erected.

BELOW: A particularly attractive bush of gorse springs into bloom along the banks of the River Duddon. Downstream of Whistling Green, below Ulpha and before the road rises to pass beneath Stonestar Crag, there is a section of open common land where the road passes in close proximity to the river. There are some lovely deep pools here and a mixture of rough pasture, craggy knoll and brackened hillside interspersed with numerous clumps of gorse.

It is a favourite place to take a picnic or a light stroll.

BELOW RIGHT: In the woods of the Lower Duddon, among the rock and flood debris left by a raging river, a golden bunch of wild indigenous Lake District daffodils stands serene and undaunted.

OPPOSITE: In March, the profusion of small wild daffodils found throughout the woods and along the banks of the Lower Duddon is one of the finest and most heartening sights of the region. This is their stronghold, for they are much reduced throughout the rest of the Lake District and are now considered rare in Britain. Look and do not touch – it is against the law to pick them. That they survive here is quite remarkable, and is probably down to the ancient fifteen-year coppice rotation employed by the nearby Duddon Iron Furnace – back in the 1800s it used to consume some 10 acres of coppice wood a week.

RIGHT: A wilder aspect of the
Duddon in early spring, looking
over Crosbythwaite from Hesk
Fell to the heights of Great Worm
Crag on the edge of Birker Fell.
The uplands are still burnt
brown, with fresh snow evident
on the Scafells beyond, but the
stone wall-enclosed pasture fields
are now green with fresh grass.

ABOVE: Above Seathwaite, where the Duddon becomes channelled through the steep confines of Wallowbarrow Gorge, bypassed unseen by the main road, there is a hanging basin of pastureland virtually enclosed by little craggy steeps. The river here is not the Duddon but Tarn Beck, having fallen down Seathwaite Fell. Like a forgotten oasis, it is both a delight to the eye and to a sense of the sublime should you happen upon it. This is a view over the basin past Long House to the craggy heights of Sunny Pike and Troutal House High Close.

OPPOSITE: Leaving the track to Seathwaite Tarn, the Walna Scar Road makes a steep, rough ascent up the side of Seathwaite Fell to cross the high col between Brown Pike and White Maiden. From here it falls to traverse the foot of mighty Coniston Old Man and so down to Coniston. It is not fit for regular motorised transport, but since it is still classed as a public road groups of motorbikes and 4x4s see it as a legitimate challenge. This is a pity, for the silence of the hills is a rare and precious commodity in this modern age. The trees and bushes on the left mark the line of Long House Gill.

ABOVE: Sycamore buds burst into leaf on the banks of the Duddon.

FAR LEFT: Sorbus aucuparia, commonly known as rowan or mountain ash, which looked lifeless and dead during the winter months, throws out its exquisite pinnate of serrated leaves.

LEFT: Still with the remnants of its creamy May blossom intact, the rowan continues its spring cycle of regeneration.

RIGHT: Shouldering the higher sycamore behind, a rowan gracefully spreads its leaves across the fast-flowing waters of the young River Duddon a little way below Cockley Beck. Brown trout will be glad of its shade and camouflage during the hot days of summer to come.

BELOW: The tops of Scafell Pike (left) and Broad Crag (centre) and Ill Crag peep over the rim of Mosedale. The good track (left) seen flanking over the brackened hillside above Mosedale Beck leads into the main basin of the little hanging valley to disappear among thick bog. Although the track now vanishes for a short section, inevitably resulting in wet feet, this is a delightful way to travel. It was once a main trackway both into the upper regions of Eskdale and up Lingcove to Ore Gap and hence down to Borrowdale, Langdale or Wasdale. For climbers, this is the main route to the Esk Buttress (locally known as Dow Crag), one of the finest climbing crags in the region, standing at the head of Upper Eskdale's Great Moss. As a child, every spring I used to walk this way with my father to investigate the nesting peregrine falcons on Cam Spout Buttress – we used to call it 'The Falconer's Path'. Thankfully Mosedale and its environs remain remote and serenely beautiful.

*ABOVE: Over the sparkling
waters of Seathwaite Tarn, the
central portion of the Duddon
is arrayed far below. The far
hills are the Whitfell group,
terminating in Black Combe
on their far left. Dotted around
the basin are numerous little
craggy outcrops which offer rock
climbing possibilities – I have
had a lot of fun and some
adventure here.*

OPPOSITE TOP: View over a low stone barn into Wrynose Bottom. Traditionally this building would have served to store hay and shelter beasts during the inhospitable months of winter.

OPPOSITE LEFT: A 'Black Lamb', using the wire fence as a convenient back rest, absorbs the sun's warmth. A 'Black Lamb' does not necessarily have to be black in colour; in local parlance the expression refers to a lamb born to a sheep that remains high on the fells and has not been gathered. Soon all the lambs born at valley level will group together and, with new-found independence and confidence, gambol in the meadows. Carefree spring lambs are one of the most heart-warming sights of the season.

OPPOSITE RIGHT: A Herdwick ewe, gathered from the fells in April to lamb at valley level, with her spring lamb.

ABOVE: Crystal-clear spring air heightens the impact of this classic image of the Duddon. In the foreground lambs graze, while silver birch become resplendent green to the left of the river swollen by recent rain. The prominent fell beyond the white building of Dale Head is Little Stand, while Mosedale runs off left into the fells.

BELOW: In the high hills near the source of the Duddon, this is a view from Black Crag on Pike o' Blisco looking over the head of the valley to Wet Side Edge, Carrs and Swirl How (seen centrally) with Grey Friar protruding to the right. It is a rugged, fascinating landscape of boulders, craggy outcrops and curious arrangements of rocks amid little tarnlets and coarse fell grass.

OPPOSITE: South-west over High Wallowbarrow Farm and the walled pastures of the mid Duddon, seen from the heights of Wallowbarrow Crag. Below the obvious triangular top of The Pike, standing above Ulpha, the valley closes once more to head south on its final leg to the sea.

LEFT: Between Dale Head and Hinning House on the upper reaches of the Duddon stands this sycamore, viewed looking downstream with Castle How out of the picture to the right.

BELOW: The same sycamore tree looking upstream with the backdrop of high fells beyond: Little Stand to the left and Cold Pike to the right. The sycamore reputedly came over from Europe with the Romans; within this region of the Lake District it is a much-loved tree. Many of the fifteenth-century farms hereabouts have stands of purposely planted sycamore. The most obvious reason is that they form strong windbreaks, but the sycamore has many other qualities. In spring, the small pale green flowers hang in clusters. Along with field maple and limes, sycamore is the only common tree with insect-pollinated flowers and is a vital source of pollen and nectar for bees. To the delight of all children, the bunches of fertilised flowers develop into winged seeds or 'helicopters'. When ripe, they spin away from the parent tree in the autumn wind or when picked and thrown into the air. When I was a child we used to make 'sycamore whistles' with our penknives. The best time for this is spring when the sap begins to flow. It involves cutting a short length of branch, sliding off the bark intact, notching the white wood, then sliding back the sleeve of bark. Suddenly you were the proud possessor of a fine, piercing whistle.

BELOW: Saxifrage beside the road as it passes Cockley Beck Farm outbuildings.

OPPOSITE: At the stone arch bridge at Cockley Beck under Harter Fell the stand of sycamore is just gaining leaf. At this point the road splits – right to climb Hardnott Pass and so to Eskdale, left to descend the Duddon.

RIGHT: A burst of sunshine through Dunnerdale Forest illuminates the rocky volcanic plug of Castle How. The little overhanging wall in shadow sports a few difficult rock climbs, though few others tread the heights of this little crag. In springtime it is the regular nesting site for a pair of peregrine falcons and is strictly off limits. Luckily for bird watchers, a perfect view can be had from the road only a few hundred metres distant.

'wonderful' walker

BELOW: Beside the entrance to Seathwaite Church this stone, complete with copper sundial and plaque, was once used by Robert Walker as a stool when he donned his sheep-shearer's hat. He would have sat on one end and placed the sheep facing the same way with its bottom on the stone, then duly clipped the woollen fleece with sheep shears. The 'Gateskell Farm' (Gaitscale Farm above Wrynose Bottom) in the inscription is now in ruins – nevertheless, local legend persists that sheep from this farm had an extra rib, to explain why they were apparently larger and longer than those from nearby farms.

BELOW: Inside Seathwaite Church is to be found this brass plaque in memory of 'Wonderful' Walker and his wife Ann.

BELOW: Seathwaite Church is wonderfully situated at the edge of the village, near the banks of Tarn Beck. The original chapel was built in the first half of the sixteenth century. In 1870 it was deemed to be in a such bad state that it was rebuilt in its present form and consecrated in May 1875. The tree on the right is a very fine yew of considerable size and antiquity under which, during the rebuilding of the church, a wedding took place on 25 August 1874. The vicarage, now a private house, stands opposite the church on the other side of the road.

summer

Ulpha Bridge is always a favourite, the deep pool below providing a refreshing welcome to those who take the plunge. Most jump feet first; the brave (or reckless) run across the road to dive over the parapet. Survivors get to laze in the sunshine on the gently sloping grass of Ulpha Common. For years, two white-bearded brothers sat in the shed doorway at the end of the bridge whittling sticks with sharp knives, nodding knowledgeably to the occasional passing motorist. They are gone, but the warmth and fragrance of each summer, the timeless charm and myriad splendour of this quiet river valley and its watchful heights remain undiminished.

OPPOSITE: The deep clear pools of the River Duddon are irresistible during the balmy days of summer. But do take care, for rocks abound and deep pools can be chillingly cold even on the hottest days – look and feel before you leap. This pool can be found just above the footbridge which crosses the bottom of Wallowbarrow Gorge.

LEFT: Sweeping through the rocky tree-lined confines of Wallowbarrow Gorge, the River Duddon is at its most vibrant. Huge rocks – this one has probably tumbled from the cliff above – create a series of tumbling waterfalls and deep pools. A narrow footpath picks a way through the rocks and mix of deciduous trees on the west bank of the river.

BELOW LEFT: Little used and seldom seen, these stepping stones cross the Duddon below Wallowbarrow Bridge. Numerous sets of such stones are to be discovered throughout the length of the Duddon, presumably predating the earliest bridges.

OPPOSITE: The mixed woods of Wallowbarrow are always enchanting; if elves exist they surely dwell here. Rather more visible, reducing the insect population and keeping the woods in good order, are the large red wood ants found here. They may disrupt your picnic, and give you a mild dose of formic acid should you show them any aggression, but they are basically harmless. The most visible signs of their presence are their large nests of twigs, which can stand over a metre high.

OVERLEAF: Early evening sunshine illuminates this view over Black Hall towards Dale Head. The neatly stone-walled pasture fields are still resplendently green though the long summer is coming to its end. In the flush of early youth, the River Duddon runs through the mid-ground.

ABOVE: A late summer view
looking up the Duddon towards
Dale Head. Contrasting with
the long golden-brown grass,
the dark green leaves on the
trees to the right are sycamore.

ABOVE: A view over the valley to Grey Friar from above the craggy outcrops that define the upper edge of Dunnerdale Forest on the slopes of Harter Fell.

LEFT: An ancient packhorse route leads along the high shoulder of Ulpha Park to cross Bleabeck Bridge on its way from Millbrow to Logan Beck Bridge. Before the track, heading south, dips behind the hill of Penn, it passes Frith Hall and offers superb views up the valley. Once in an area of considerable enterprise, this route undoubtedly served many diverse industries. Below Millbrow, at the bottom of the hill, still stand the buildings of the Ulpha Bobbin Mill, last used c. 1902. It started life much earlier, being ideally sited to tap the water power from Holehouse Beck. Nearby Rainsbarrow Wood was once harvested for its considerable crop of hazelnuts. Logan Beck was the site of a waulking mill, where wool was processed before it was made into clothes – the Cistercian monks of Furness Abbey organised a thriving wool industry in the region back in the thirteenth century. On the hills above are numerous copper workings.

ABOVE RIGHT: Upstream of Hall Bridge stand the cottages of Bridge End, built during the Napoleonic wars by shoemaker James Dawson. The pagoda-type building on the river side of the road, visible left of the tall bush, once sheltered a petrol pump – when I was a lad I remember getting my tank filled up with petrol here by hand pump. James Dawson Junior (great grandson of the above) put in the petrol pumps and operated a light engineering works from the wooden part of the building, making fishing tackle and tying his own flies. It was here, in 1936, that he caught a 26lb salmon. His daughters operated the petrol pump until 1978 and until very recently kept the memory of the famous salmon alive by refreshing its outline (see page 85).

RIGHT: The double stone arch of Seathwaite Bridge still carries the main road over Tarn Beck. Harter Fell, ever present in the upper half of the valley, stands beyond.

LEFT: Leaving the Duddon in the direction of Dunnerdale via the road over Kiln Bank, you pass one of the most remarkable stone walls in the Lake District. The stones employed are simply huge. How did the builders lift and place them? Another mystery, or is it a clue? – if you look into the steep field behind there is a ruinous wall, of equally gigantic stones, running up the hillside to a platform-like structure. Who built this, when and why? Maybe they are something to do with the kilns that gave the name to this bank.

ABOVE: Two good-looking ponies in the field below Hall Dunnerdale. In times past, this field may well have had many such animals waiting for their next task – ponies were the mainstay of the local economy, providing the only means of transport for the many industries operating in the area. Traditionally, they would have been the long-haired, good-natured Lakeland fell ponies, which reputedly were derived from horse stock brought over by the Romans.

ABOVE: All around the valley, though quietly disappearing (perhaps to agricultural museum collections), are the remains of long-abandoned farm machinery. In this hay meadow, at the front of Hinning House, are the remnants of two old horse-drawn mowing machines which were probably engineered locally. Like some Indian totem poles sticking up into the sky, with Little Stand forming the backdrop, the upright is the cutting edge that worked scissor-like to crop the grass. The favourite shire horse in these parts was the hard-working, mild-mannered, intelligent, wonderful Clydesdale. When I was a lad I had the good fortune to work – probably 'laik' (play) would be more accurate – on Wilson Place Farm, which still used a working Clydesdale. That is an experience you can never forget.

ABOVE: Even in summer the view along Wrynose Bottom can look wild and desolate.

BELOW: The upper tracts of the
Duddon looking to Dale Head.
Cleared and cultivated pasture
gives way to rougher ground
within the flood plain of the river.

LEFT AND OPPOSITE: The peacock butterfly, arguably the most spectacular of all Lakeland's butterflies, enjoys the last of the summer sunshine in early September. Beside the path from Seathwaite to Wallowbarrow were a great number of these butterflies inhabiting a colony of sheepsbit (a flower known as 'blue buttons' in the old county of Cumberland). They made for an amazingly colourful scene in miniature and photographically I was spoilt for choice – which is far from the norm when attempting to capture this elusive insect.

LEFT: A five-petal white blackberry, or bramble, flower. Later in the season, transformation will be made into the familiar succulent fruit much loved by children of all ages.

ABOVE: High on the shoulder of Ulpha Park, occupying a commanding position above the lower section of the Duddon, stand the ruins of Frith Hall. Seen from the road – gaunt, black and sinister against the sky – it draws the eye and fuels the imagination. Up close it is no less powerful and impressive. It has had a long and colourful history and is thought locally to be haunted. It is supposed to have been built in about the twelfth century as a hunting lodge to accompany the Norman deer park now known as Ulpha Park. Later there is evidence that it was fortified in the manner of a pele tower. Defeat of the King's men by the Roundheads in c. 1640 brought an end to Frith Hall as a lodge, and by the mid 1700s it had become an inn. It acquired a reputation for wildness and lawlessness and was the centre of smuggling exploits. Runaway marriages were performed here – in 1730 some seventeen of them. On 10 October 1736, still talked about locally, came the murder of 'sojourner' William Marshall; he was buried on the spot, and naturally his ghost still haunts Frith Hall. Some hundred years later the hall was being used as a farm; it fell into disuse and ruin around 1830.

OPPOSITE: Frith Hall set romantically against the background of high fells surrounding the head of the Duddon. This is the view taken from the old packhorse route, an important track which was subsequently widened to take horse-drawn coaches.

LEFT: Ulpha Bridge has timeless appeal.

ABOVE: The view from Millbrow over Ulpha with the River Duddon masked by trees. The shapely peak top right is Caw (Calf) Peak, with the Coniston Fells seen beyond.

OVERLEAF: A red-hot sun breaks through a bank of purple cloud over the upper Duddon, looking to Harter Fell (left), the col of Hardnott Pass (centre) and Border End (right).

journey of the salmon

Atlantic salmon make a great journey from the salty Atlantic to the freshwater rivers and streams of their birth. Once in the freshwater of the River Duddon they develop distinctive mating colours. Males, known as cock salmon, also grow hooked jaws to compete for females. The females, known as hens, select a fast-flowing part of the river, preferably a gravel bed, where high oxygen levels make it easier for eggs and young fish to develop. The hen prepares a breeding place, a redd, by flicking her tail in the gravel, before a cock joins her and the two fish release eggs and sperm together. The whole cycle is so exhausting that many fish die after spawning and only some 10 per cent (mainly hens) survive to return to the sea.

Levels of salmon (and sea trout) spawning in the Duddon are now dangerously low; stringent restrictions apply to those fishing with rod and line within the permitted season and some fish must be returned to the water. Once the River Duddon and the estuary were famed for the quality and numbers of salmon, sea trout, eels and cockles. Salmon were salted or smoked and stored in barrels. They were so common that apprentices employed at the Ulpha Bobbin Mill, fed by their employers, had a clause in their contracts stating that they were *not* to be given salmon to eat more than three days a week. How times change!

ABOVE: Superbly camouflaged among the dappled waters and rocks of this high pool, a lone cock salmon waits to fertilise the eggs of a hen. Yes, you can see it – it is lying, tail between two dark rocks, dead centre of this photograph. Although they 'run' throughout the year, autumn is the most important time for the migration of both salmon and sea trout from sea and estuary to the high spawning grounds of the River Duddon.

ABOVE RIGHT: Having been removed by the ancient art of tickling (just to keep our hand in!) this fish is being returned to the river unharmed. Apart from its being illegal to remove sea trout or salmon without rod and licence (a custodial sentence can be the result for anyone poaching), there are so few fish these days that any taken would seem to be a threat to their survival.

BELOW: A typical spawning pool high in the Duddon, reached by both salmon and sea trout. Few appreciate just how far upstream these fish travel in their return to traditional spawning grounds – a huge physical effort against, alternately, raging torrent and low water levels insufficient to swim through. So should you picnic beside the river, before you throw stones have a thought for the fish fighting for their survival somewhere in a pool near you.

RIGHT: Atop the wall in front of Bridge End is the outline, enhanced with chalk, of a great 26lb salmon caught by James Dawson on 19 August 1936, using rod and tackle he made himself. A wooden fly reel and box of handmade flies, tied by my grandfather, indicate the scale.

autumn

We call it 'backend' – when the leaves begin to colour and fall. In between downpours it's the time when the run of silver sea trout is most prolific. So well camouflaged, with their dark green to black backs blending perfectly with the river's stony bed, they are to the inexperienced eye almost impossible to see. Your best chance is when one turns and twists to snap at a passing submerged leaf – a momentary flash of silver in some deep green pool as it exposes its lighter underbelly. Instinctively, salmon know their way from the estuary to the high spawning grounds. Their rite of passage has been followed long before the first tourist gazed in awe or Wordsworth dabbled his baited line, before iron ore was converted at Duddon Bridge Furnace, or the charcoal burner felled the coppices and the monks of Furness tended the earth, before the Norsemen glided silently from sea to river and the Romans tramped along Wrynose Bottom, before even the ancients stood crowded around the stone circle of Swinside.

OPPOSITE: *Above Hall Dunnerdale a twin-trunked oak colours stridently against a dark sky.*

BELOW: With the leaves blown from the ash and silver birch, as a storm gathers behind, rusty brown Herdwick tup hogs graze below Cockley Beck Farm. They are first-year rams and winter will soon be upon them. Though it is only a few months ago that they gambolled carefree beside their mothers as black and white lambs, it now seems a long time ago.

OPPOSITE: Highlights of copper-coloured beech flank this view looking to Low Hall, Hall Dunnerdale and the pastel heights of Wallowbarrow Crag in the darkening beyond: autumn in the mid Duddon.

OPPOSITE TOP LEFT: Turning from green to orange-red, the wonderfully coloured leaves of the red oak by Hinning House are more commonly seen in North America. It is a welcome contributor to the Duddon's autumn tapestry. The leaves are conspicuous by their deep, finely pointed lobes.

OPPOSITE TOP RIGHT: The little hazel, slight as it is, is one of the most influential trees or shrubs in the landscape of the Duddon. Once important as a coppice wood, the hazel remains the mainstay for making the traditional shepherd's crook. In autumn before the leaves turn to delicate yellow they hang with nuts – in times past, these were considered a worthwhile commercial crop in this enterprising valley.

OPPOSITE BELOW: On the fringe of the magical woods of the Duddon, this path leads to High Wallowbarrow Farm.

RIGHT: Beyond the gate, hazel, silver birch and oak beckon. Who could resist the call of Duddon's famous woods?

BELOW: Below Wallowbarrow
Gorge and the village of
Seathwaite is the confluence
of the Duddon and Tarn Beck.
Already majestic, the river
becomes even greater. The
heather-clad and brackened
flanks of rocky Wallowbarrow
Crag can be seen beyond the
pool and hanging bows of oak.

BELOW: 'Backend' (autumn) in the Duddon, looking up the river from Hinning House, with the edge of Dunnerdale Forest flanking Harter Fell to the left, and the white farmhouse of Dale Head to the right. The lonely little valley of Mosedale breaks off left beneath the high fells of Little Stand, Crinkle Crags and Bowfell on the far left. Most of the leaves have gone from the trees yet wonderful colour lingers beside the river. Although this scene epitomises the peace and quiet of the valley, traditionally this is one of the busiest times of the year for the river, with the run of sea trout and salmon from the estuary to the spawning grounds at its height.

BELOW: The rocky island of Hollin House Haw with the old farm of Under Crag, birthplace of 'Wonderful' Walker, nestling beneath to its right

OPPOSITE: Autumn colours over the mid Duddon seen from Kiln Bank. Beyond are the heights of Scafell and to the left the serrated rocky tops of Green Crag forming the eastern edge of Birker Fell.

OPPOSITE TOP: Rosehips set against a blue sky. When the petals of the wild rose fall, the hips are left – a rich source of Vitamin C, harvested and made into tea by the resourceful folk of the Duddon.

OPPOSITE BELOW LEFT: Crimson rowan berries near Troutal, perfect for rowan jelly.

OPPOSITE BELOW RIGHT: Purple bell heather enjoying the sun on Stonestar Crag: aromatic winter bedding.

ABOVE: Near Troutal Gorge a beech drops its leaves into the Duddon.

OVERLEAF: Down the Duddon valley the sun drops over the flanks of Grey Friar, with Harter Fell standing centrally.

BELOW: Lined by trees between Turner Hall Farm and Seathwaite Church, Tarn Beck rushes down a rocky channel to crash over a series of waterfalls.

OPPOSITE TOP LEFT: Stems with bulbous bottoms turning from scarlet to faint yellow, with broad cushion caps of light grey and undersides (tubes) of light yellow, reveal this to be Boletus calopus. Reputedly it is inedible due to a bitter taste, and causes stomach and abdominal pains. So it is not quite so nice as it looks! This example was growing beside the river in the beech woods beneath Fickle Crag on the path from Grassguards.

OPPOSITE TOP CENTRE: Found by Birks Bridge, this fly agaric, spectacular in colour and form despite being shrunken and aged, is the classic toadstool. Powerfully hallucinogenic, it is highly poisonous, containing compounds so complex they have not yet been analysed. Apparently the Vikings used its properties prior to battle to give them a feeling of strength and invincibility.

OPPOSITE TOP RIGHT: Growing as it should below a silver birch tree is this birch bolete. The young mushrooms are extremely palatable.

OPPOSITE BELOW LEFT: My local expert informs me that is a false chanterelle and therefore inedible, unlike the real thing which is among the tastiest of all mushrooms.

OPPOSITE BELOW CENTRE: Next to a quartz-infused boulder on Hollin House Tongue, I found this gold-coloured toadstool which looked for all the world as though someone had just sprayed it with paint. It could be a glistening ink cap, and is probably inedible

OPPOSITE BELOW RIGHT: Hard, scaly and poisonous, Inonotus radiatus is found on living alder trees which it kills rather quickly.

BELOW: Elegant beech woods extend down the hillside from Fickle Crag to the Duddon and a rich variety of fungi can be found here during autumn. Indeed, throughout the diverse woods of the Duddon there are many species. Do have a care if you collect or pick fungi: many are inedible and a few are deadly poisonous with no known or effective antidote – notably death cap and the destroying angel. You must be absolutely certain that what you pick is safe to eat.

BELOW: At Birks Bridge the river level in the narrow rock channel seems far below the arch, but in times of spate it rises to bridge level. The line of circular drain holes in the stone parapet above the arch are to allow the floodwaters through so that the bridge is not washed away by the force of the water. At this time of year, salmon may be seen queuing in the long pool, waiting for the water to rise sufficiently to allow their passage up the waterfall above the bridge.

LEFT: A small tortoiseshell butterfly alights on a bunch of ragwort among the walls of the ruined farm at Nettle Slack below and to the south of High Tongue.

BELOW LEFT: A dung beetle takes a stroll – this is the Dor which lives in cow dung.

BELOW RIGHT: A hairy caterpillar wraps itself defensively around a stalk of grass.

OPPOSITE: Low Stonythwaite lies in a fold in the hills beside Wallowbarrow Crag. Once a small farmstead, it was recently renovated for holiday accommodation but can still be reached only by a high, rough track that passes through Grassguards.

ABOVE: High above the Duddon Estuary, Swinside Stone Circle is thought to be Neolithic and is one of the oldest circles in the region. The standing stones are tightly grouped and the arrangement almost perfectly circular, making it most impressive. It is also known as Sunkenkirk from an early attempt to explain the origin of the stones: legend has it that one night the Devil caused a church (kirk) to sink into the ground.

OPPOSITE: Above Wrynose Bottom, on the flanks of Little Stand, Gaitscale Farm appears green among the brown bracken. There are numerous buildings, walls and enclosures associated with the ruins and distinct areas of raised earthworks. Because of the extent of the ruins and the proximity of the Roman road traversing the foot of the area, it is tempting to think that some of the remains are Roman in origin. As far as I am aware, no

archaeological work has been done on the site. We know that 'Wonderful' Walker clipped sheep here some time in the middle of the 1700s, and it is suspected that the farm was abandoned in the first half of the 1800s.

rock features

BELOW: Hippo Rock can be found by the upper section of path which rises initially by the edge of Dunnerdale Forest, up the south-west nose of Harter Fell. A good approach to this path can be made from the end of the forestry track that rises above Grassguards.

RIGHT: The climb is 'Pocket Wall' on Black Crag on the flanks of Pike o' Blisco, and the climber Dave Birkett. The volcanic rock here is very distinctively marked with pockets and oval 'plaques'.

OPPOSITE TOP: A ring of rocky outcrops, cut through by a deep corridor, make the summit of pyramidal Harter Fell one of the most fascinating in the Lake District. It is thought that this prominent top once served as a Roman signalling station. Looking towards the Scafells, George Sharpe admires the view, arguably the finest in the region, while enjoying a flask of Lapsang Souchong tea.

OPPOSITE BELOW LEFT: Rimed with frost, this pile of boulders is to be found next to Cockley Beck along Wrynose Bottom. Is it natural or arranged by man?

OPPOSITE BELOW RIGHT: A closer view of the tumbled rocks below Black Crag show their intriguing marks, here more circular than oval. Known as 'oddball concretions', they are thought to have formed around fragments of volcanic rock fired into layers of volcanic ash. The layers of ash subsequently formed the mother rock.

index